Who's That Face?

Using Principles of Human Heredity in Photograph

Identification

By **Donovan Hurst**

March 14, 2014

Dedication

This work is dedicated to all of those that came before us and shaped our lives to make us the people that we are today.

Table of Contents

Abstract

This work provides insight on how to use genetic principles in identifying family photographs, which can also be used with the identification of other types of images found on Carte de Visites (CDVs), Ambrotypes, Daguerreotypes, Tintypes, Cabinet Cards, etc. The author illustrates his points by using photographs from his own personal collection.

Introduction

For family history researchers it is important to be aware of the basic fundamental concepts of human heredity. At the cellular level each person contains DNA (deoxyribonucleic acid), which is comprised of genes that make us who we are. Genes can either be dominant or recessive. Dominant genes are expressed in each of the subsequent generations. Recessive genes are expressed in every other subsequent generation. If the gene for brown hair was a dominant gene, you would expect the potential offspring in each subsequent generation to have brown hair. If the gene for non-brown hair was a recessive gene, you would expect that the potential offspring in the second generation to have non-brown hair. Another way to see how dominant and recessive genes operate is to create a Punnett Square. For this example, we will use a "B" to represent the dominant gene for brown hair and a "b" to represent the recessive gene for non-brown hair. The male parent will be homozygous dominant, containing two dominant genes, and the female parent will be homozygous recessive, containing two recessive genes.

Who's that Face?

	Mom b	Mom b
Dad B	Bb	Bb
Dad B	Bb	Bb

The potential offspring will be heterozygous, containing one dominant gene and one recessive gene, with the dominant gene being expressed resulting in four potential offspring with brown hair. However each of the four potential offspring will be capable of having offspring that could have non-brown hair because they contain the recessive gene.

Using Principles of Human Heredity on Photograph Identification

Now let us look at what happens when the male and female parent will be heterozygous, containing one dominant and one recessive gene.

	Mom B	Mom b
Dad B	BB	Bb
Dad b	Bb	bb

The potential offspring will have a 25% chance of being homozygous (dominant), containing two dominant genes, a 25 % chance of being homozygous (recessive), containing two recessive genes, and a 50% chance of being heterozygous, containing one dominant gene and one recessive gene, resulting in three out of the four potential offspring with the dominant gene being expressed and one of the four potential offspring with the recessive gene being expressed. Therefore, if four children were born, three of the four children will have brown hair and one of the children will have non-brown hair.

No two people are the same with genes being contributed from each parent, who have had genes contributed to them from each of their parents. If you start with yourself and go back 3 generations to your great-grandparents, then you have genetic material coming from 14 different people. Keep this fact in mind when you are observing genetic traits in photographs because a trait that you observe in one of your parents, might well have come from their grandparents and not one of their parents. The genes contained in a person provide for the expression of various genetic traits or characteristics. For example each person expresses different traits such as height, weight, skin complexion, hair color, eye color, eye shape, ear shape, nose shape, lip shape, and various internal traits only seen by medical professionals with the use of tests. Even though no two people are the same, the child should express genetic traits of either their father or mother. Have you not heard the following expression before, "He has his mother's eyes." However, when observing the child and no genetic traits seem to come from either the father or mother, remember the traits could have come from any number of the father's ancestors or the mother's ancestors. From my own personal family

Using Principles of Human Heredity on Photograph Identification

experience, I have noticed that, even though each of my siblings and me resemble genetic traits in our parents and grandparents, each of my siblings resemble genetic traits for a specific ancestral line. My oldest sister resembles genetic traits from my father's father side of the family, my brother resembles genetic traits from my mother's father side of the family, my next oldest sister resembles genetic traits from my father's mother side of the family, and I resemble genetic traits from my mother's mother side of the family. While looking for similar genetic traits in your photographs, be aware that genetic traits can be recessive and expressed later in another generation. For example, the genetic trait causing baldness skips a generation. It does not matter if your father was not bald, but if either of your grandfathers were bald. Your chances of becoming bald could be higher than someone whose grandparents were not bald. Of course there is a wide array of genetic traits, but the easiest genetic traits to observe when looking at photographic images concern the individual's head and face. Pay close attention to the person's shape of their head, hair line, jaw line, eyes, nose, lips, and ears.

To illustrate how genetic traits can be observed in photographs I will use images from my own family collection, which have been passed down from my great-grandmother Sadie Anita Cecelia (Nelson) Calkins to prove that one

Who's that Face?

photograph was mislabeled. Here follows a brief description of the lineage of the individuals I will be discussing in this example:

- **William Arthur Calkins** married to **Sadie Anita Cecelia Nelson** (Author's great-grandparents)

- **William Riley Calkins** married to **Mary Etta Perry**, parents of **William Arthur Calkins**.

- **Freeman Calkins** married to **Sarah Ann Woods**, parents of **William Riley Calkins**.

Image 1

Freeman Calkins & Sarah Ann Woods

Using Principles of Human Heredity on Photograph Identification

Image 1 was always told to our family as William Riley Calkins and Mary Etta Perry, the parents of my great-grandfather William Arthur Calkins. The photograph was a copy of the original photograph, which was made by the youngest daughter of Sadie Anita Cecelia (Nelson) Calkins with writing identifying the individuals on the back of the photograph. The writing was made by two different people with two different pens, one black ink, which stated, "Maryetta Perry Calkins [Top Line] Wm Riley Calkins [Bottom Line with ditto marks written instead of Calkins] and one red ink, which stated, "William Arthur Calkins Parents". I was always curious about if the photograph was mislabeled because of the two sets of writing, but with no other photographs to use as a reference guide photograph; I accepted the photograph for my great-grandfather's parents.

Who's that Face?

Image 2

William Riley Calkins, holding William Arthur Calkins, and Mary Etta Perry holding Mabel Effie Calkins.

Image 2 was shared with our family from one of my grandaunts and oldest daughter of Sadie Anita Cecelia (Nelson) Calkins about a couple of years before her passing. The photograph had no writing on the back identifying the individuals in the photograph. The photograph was taken in O'Neill, Nebraska as stated on the photograph's front, which listed the name and location of the photographer. The image contained a man and woman, with a toddler sized boy seated on the man's lap and an infant held by the woman.

Using Principles of Human Heredity on Photograph Identification

From the previous research[1] I had conducted on the Calkins Family associated with our family, I was able to conclude that the man and woman was William Riley Calkins and his wife Mary Etta Perry holding their two youngest children, William Arthur Calkins and Mabel Effie Calkins.

This was exciting for me because I had only seen the one picture, Image 1, and now here was another picture. I placed the two photographs side by side and started to compare the two men and two women. To my surprise I saw differences in each of the four individuals causing me to question the identity of the man and woman from Image 1 that I was told was William Riley Calkins and Mary Etta Perry. I proceeded by making digital copies of each image, which I could view more easily on my computer monitor. From my new digital files I created additional images to be compared.

---

[1] See the work entitled <u>Elisha Calkins & Anna Dalrymple Descendants</u> by Donovan Hurst

Who's that Face?

Image 3

Freeman Calkins

Image 4

William Riley Calkins

Using Principles of Human Heredity on Photograph Identification

Image 5

Sarah Ann Woods

Image 6

Mary Etta Perry

Who's that Face?

I began with the two men in Images 3 & 4. Overall the two heads and faces appear to be similar. However, the shape of the eyes differs between the two images. The shape of the nose is narrow on Image 3 with the shape of the nose being wider on Image 4. The shape of the jaw line appears more squared on Image 3, where as the shape of the jaw line appears more rounded on Image 4. The top of the skull on Image 3 is more curved from the top of the skull and then goes straight towards the ear, where as the top of the skull on Image 4 bends inward and out towards the ear.

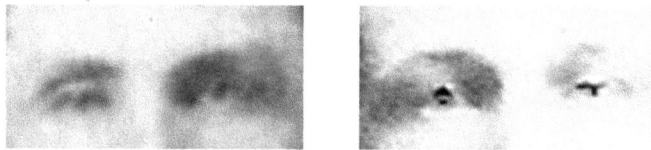

Image 7

Close up of Eyes

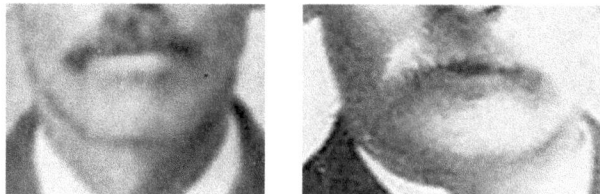

Image 8

Close up of Jaw Line

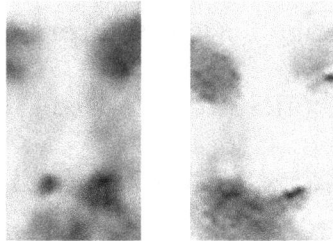

Image 9

Close up of Nose

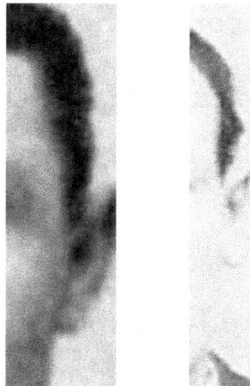

Image 10

Close up of shape towards Top of Skull

Who's that Face?

I had already concluded that the man in Image 4 was William Riley Calkins. If the person in Image 3 was different then the person in Image 4, but were related, I logically concluded that the man in Image 3 was Freeman Calkins the father of William Riley Calkins. If this was true then the woman in Image 5 would be Sarah Ann Woods the wife of Freeman Calkins. Image 1 then is the grandparents to William Arthur Calkins and not his parents.

Once I concluded that Image 1, Image 3, and Image 5 were the parents of William Riley Calkins, I began comparing William Riley Calkins, Image 4, with his parents using Images 3 & 5 in order to see which traits William Riley Calkins expressed from each of his parents. If my conclusion was correct, certain traits of William Riley Calkins should match or at least be extremely similar to those traits expressed by each of his parents. I noticed there were similarities between the parents and their son. For example, the skull shape from the top of the skull to the ear is similar between mother and son shown in Images 5 & 4, where as the general shape of the jaw line is similar between father and son shown in Images 3 & 4.

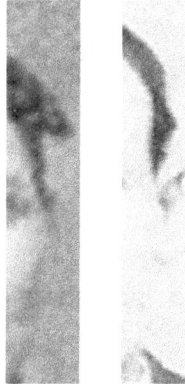

Image 11

Close up of shape towards Top of Skull

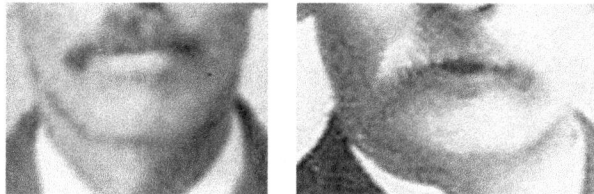

Image 12

Close up of Jaw Line

Who's that Face?

In order to make sure I was correct I looked at the two images of the women, Images 5 & 6. Two distinct differences can be found in regards to the shape of the top of skull to the ear and the shape of the ear. The top of the skull on Image 5 bends inward and out towards the ear, where as the top of the skull on Image 6 is more rounded from the top of the skull to the ear. The length of the ear on Image 5 is longer than the length of the ear on Image 6. Also the shape of the eyes is different between the two women. In Image 5 the eyes are larger, where as in Image 6 the eyes are smaller and appearing almost cat-like.

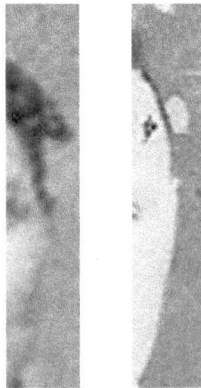

Image 13

Close up of shape towards Top of Skull

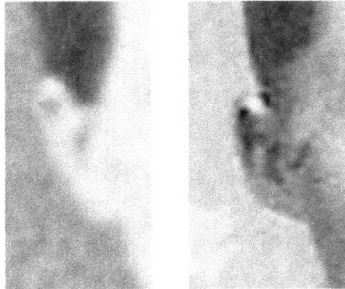

Image 14

Close up of Ear

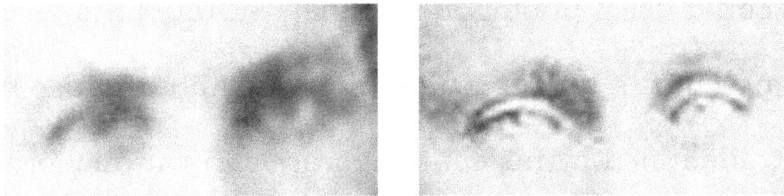

Image 15

Close up of Eyes

Clearly they are not the same individual. Using the knowledge of the fundamental concepts of human heredity and the power of observation concerning the individuals in Images 1 & 2, it is clear that the two men and two women are four completely different people.

Reference Guide Photographs

With understanding the fundamental concepts of human heredity, it will now be possible to begin working with family photographs to identify the individuals in the images, by using a reference guide photograph. The term reference guide photograph refers to a photograph in which the individual or individuals in the photograph are known to the observer. Reference guide photographs can be of any person who has been positively identified. For example, you could use a photograph of the 1st United States President George Washington as a reference guide photograph because his image has been positively identified by his contemporaries in various forms of artwork, which include paintings and sculptures. Also you could use a photograph of yourself as a reference guide photograph because you know that the person in the photograph is you. You will be able to compare the photograph of yourself to any other photograph in your family collection to see what genetic traits are similar between you and the other individuals.

Start by comparing your photograph with a photograph of each of your parents. Look for similarities in the shape of your head, hair line, jaw line, eyes, nose, lips, and ears with that of each of your parents. Does the shape of your eyes closely match your father or your mother? Does the shape of your

nose closely match your father or your mother? Continue answering those

types of questions for each genetic trait that you can observe in the

photograph. By doing this you should be able to gain a sense of if your

genetic traits are coming from your father's side of the family or your mother's

side of the family. Next compare your photograph with photographs of each of

your grandparents. This should give you a clearer idea of if your genetic traits

are coming from your father's side of the family or your mother's side of the

family. Once you are able to observe which genetic traits you have that are

coming from your father's side of the family or mother's side of the family, you

can then compare your photograph with other photographs of individuals that

have the same surname. For example, if you have traits from your father's

side of the family, whose last name is Smith; you will be able to look at

pictures of various individuals with the last name of Smith to see which

genetic traits of the last name of Smith are present in your family. Each set of

individuals that make up the genetic population for the last name Smith, who

have common ancestors will have certain genetic traits that are passed down

to the subsequent generations. For example, here are four individuals with

the last name of Smith, who are unrelated except in surname only.

Image 16

Carroll Earll Smith (Left) & Charles E. Smith (Right)

Image 17

James T. Smith (Left) & William Henry Harrison Smith (Right)

Using Principles of Human Heredity on Photograph Identification

By observing these four individuals, one can observe similar genetic traits involving the overall shape of the skull, the shape of the eyes, and the shape of the nose. With these similarities, it seems possible that these four men could share a common ancestor. Further research into each of their family historical backgrounds would be needed to validate this possibility of a shared ancestor.

Genetic traits from the earliest known ancestor for a specific family line will be passed down from generation to generation. In other words each set of individuals that make up the genetic population for a specific surname, who have common ancestors will have certain genetic traits that are passed down to the subsequent generations. It is quite possible that an individual, who is of 10th generational descent from the earliest known ancestor could look like that earliest know ancestor. For example, you could look like your 3rd great-grandparent, who in turn looked like their 3rd great-grandparent and so on until the earliest known ancestor is reached. To illustrate this point I will use images of my 3rd great-granduncle William Riley Calkins and his great-grandfather Stephen Calkins.

Who's that Face?

Image 18

William Riley Calkins

Image 19

Stephen Calkins

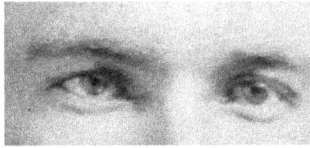

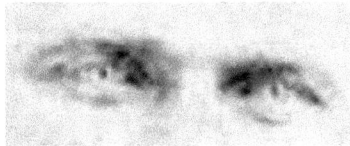

Image 20

Close up of Eyes

Image 21

Comparison of Stephen Calkins with 3rd great-grandchild

Who's that Face?

Notice the similarities between the shape of the skull, eyes, nose, mouth, and chin in each of the two images. At a quick glance you could assume that they are the same individual. Specifically looking at the shape of the eyes of each individual, a clear line of genetic inheritance is apparent. Each eye has the same shape with the only difference being the shape of the eyebrows. The eyebrow of William Riley Calkins continues straight over the eye socket, when the eyebrow of Stephen Calkins curves downward following the line of the eye socket.

Using an example of individuals that do share a common ancestor, it is possible to see how certain genetic traits have been passed down from the common ancestor to the subsequent generations. This example will use four men with the last name of Perry, one of them being the Elisha A. Perry, who is the father of Mary Etta Perry (see Images 2 & 6) and the 7th generation from the immigrant ancestor Edmund Perry. These four men are descended from Edmund Perry, who was born in Devonshire, England, about 1630. Edmund Perry immigrated to the colony at Plymouth, Massachusetts around 1660.

Image 22

Albert Perry (Left) & Elisha A. Perry (Right)

Image 23

Otis Perry (Left) & William F. Perry (Right)

Who's that Face?

By observing these four individuals, one can see similar genetic traits involving the overall shape of the skull, the shape of the eyes, the shape of the nose, and the shape of the mouth. With these similarities it is clear that these three men come from a common ancestor.

When using members of an immediate family, it should be possible to observe some dominant traits from the common ancestor being passed down through the subsequent generations. Although more difficult to observe, it is possible to observe some recessive traits from the common ancestor being passed down through the subsequent generations. Observation of these recessive traits depends on how many images are available of each of the family members from each of the subsequent generations from the common ancestor.

Let us continue discussing the occurrence of genetic traits from a common ancestor by looking at the immediate family of Elisha A. Perry, including his parents, Seth Perry & Ruba Unknown (Her surname has not be established, but there is strong possibility that it is also Perry), and uncle, Benjamin Perry. Here follows a brief description of the lineage of the individuals I will be discussing in this example:

- **Elisha A. Perry**, son of **Seth Perry** and **Ruba Unknown** (Author's 3rd great-grandfather)

- **Benjamin Perry**, brother to **Seth Perry**.

Image 24

Seth Perry & Ruba Unknown

Who's that Face?

Image 25

Elisha A. Perry

Image 26

Benjamin Perry

Image 27

Father & Son Comparison

Image 28

Uncle & Nephew Comparison

Who's that Face?

By observing the son, Image 25, with the father, Image 24, similar genetic traits can be observed in regards to the general shape of the skull, the shape of the eyes, and the shape of the mouth. However, when observing the nephew, Image 25, with the uncle, Image 26, very similar genetic traits can be observed in regard to the general shape of the skull, the shape of the eyes, and the shape of the mouth. Without a doubt specific genetic traits from the common ancestor have been expressed in each of the uncle and the nephew.

Another example of the occurrence of genetic traits from a common ancestor can be seen by looking at the immediate family of William Riley Calkins, who is the husband of Mary Etta Perry (see Images 2 & 6), including his parents, Freeman Calkins & Sarah Ann Woods, and uncle, William Riley Calkins, who also happens to share the same name. Here follows a brief description of the lineage of the individuals I will be discussing in this example:

- **William Riley Calkins**, son of **Freeman Calkins** and **Sarah Ann Woods** (Author's 2nd great-grandfather)
- **William Riley Calkins**, brother to **Freeman Calkins**.

Image 29

Freeman Calkins & Sarah Ann Woods

Image 30

William Riley Calkins

Image 31

William Riley Calkins

Image 32

Father & Son Comparison

Image 33

Mother & Son Comparison

Image 34

Uncle & Nephew Comparison

Who's that Face?

By observing the son, Image 30, with the father, Image 29, similar genetic traits can be observed in regards to the general shape of the skull, the shape of the eyes, and the shape of the mouth. When observing the son, Image 30, with the mother, Image 29, similarities can be seen in the shape of the eyes and the shape of the ears. However when observing the nephew, Image 30, with the uncle, Image 31, very similar genetic traits can be observed in regard to the general shape of the skull, the shape of the eyes, and the shape of the mouth. It is clear to see that specific genetic traits from the common ancestor have been expressed in each of the uncle and the nephew.

Transmission of Genetic Traits

Each person's dominant or recessive genetic traits are contributed from each one of their parents, who have had genes contributed to them from each one of their parents, and so on until the earliest known common ancestor is reached. Think about this statement again, "If you start with yourself and go back 3 generations to your great grandparents, then you have genetic material coming from 14 different people". That means that you have the potential to express one of fourteen combinations of genetic traits from individuals making up your parents, grandparents, great grandparents, and even earlier ancestors. You could potentially have your great grandfather's nose, your grandmother's ears, and your father's eyes, just to name a few genetic traits. This is important to remember when observing the genetic traits of individuals in photographs. Not all the traits will be transmitted or expressed and the individual in the photograph may be expressing traits transmitted from an earlier generation. It is important to use a reference guide photograph, when trying to identify genetic traits transmitted from each of the preceding family generations.

Who's that Face?

An individual person's genetic traits are transmitted from either the father's, or paternal, side of the family or the mother's, or maternal, side of the family. The following example will show how genetic traits can be transmitted from the maternal side of a family using an example of a genetic trait for the shape of the ear. The genetic trait for the shape of the ear is present in three generations of the family. Here follows a brief description of the lineage of the individuals I will be discussing in this example:

- **James Werdna Calkins** (Author's great-granduncle)

- **William Riley Calkins** married to **Mary Etta Perry**, parents of **James Werdna Calkins**.

- **Freeman Calkins** married to **Sarah Ann Woods**, parents of **William Riley Calkins**.

- **Artemas Woods** married to **Betsy Wood**, parents of **Sarah Ann Woods**.

Image 35

Artemas Woods

Image 36

Sarah Ann Woods

Who's that Face?

Image 37

William Riley Calkins

Image 38

James Werdna Calkins

Notice the shape of the right and left ears on each of the four individuals. Each ear can be described as curved, and slightly protruding. Although, the structure of each ear is similar, each ear varies slightly, due to the fact that there are an unknown number of ancestors, who have contributed their genetic material to Artemas Woods, the individual representing the earliest ancestor in the above example.

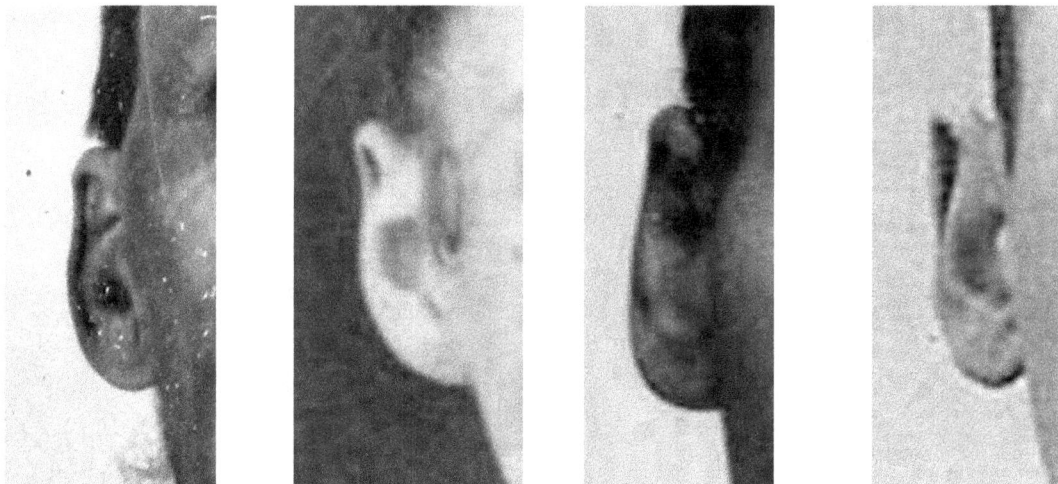

Image 39

Close up of Right Ears

(Left to Right): Artemas Woods, Sarah Ann Woods, William Riley Calkins, and James Werdna Calkins

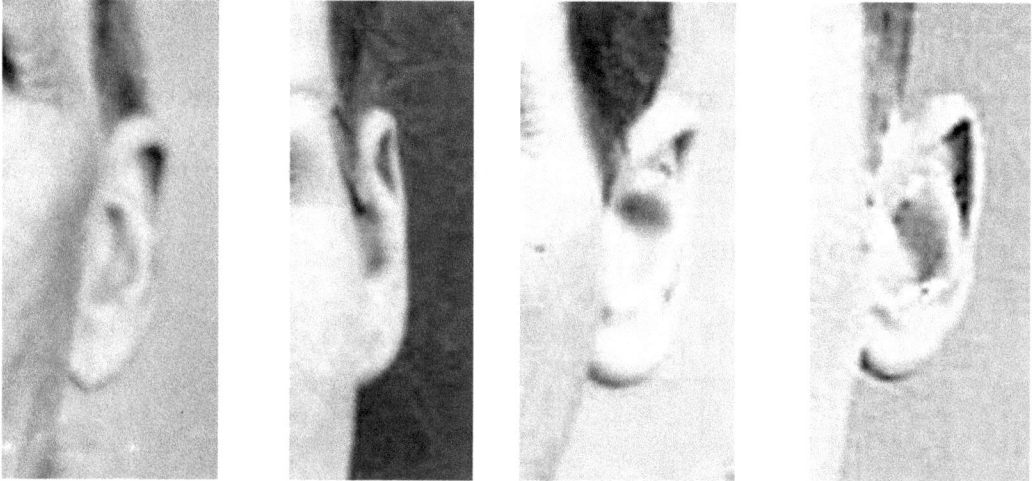

Image 40

Close up of Left Ears

(Left to Right): Artemas Woods, Sarah Ann Woods, William Riley Calkins, and James Werdna Calkins

Now that it was shown how genetic traits can be transmitted from the maternal side of a family using an example of a genetic trait for the shape of the ear, let us look at how genetic traits can be transmitted from the paternal side of the family and appear to skip a generation. Looking at Delbert C. Calkins, an older brother to James Werdna Calkins (used in the previous example), it can be observed that he resembles his grandfather Freeman Calkins more so than his father William Riley Calkins. Here follows a brief description of the lineage of the individuals I will be discussing in this example:

- **Delbert C. Calkins** (Author's great-granduncle)
- **William Riley Calkins** married to **Mary Etta Perry**, parents of **Delbert C. Calkins**.
- **Freeman Calkins** married to **Sarah Ann Woods**, parents of **William Riley Calkins**.

Who's that Face?

Image 41

Freeman Calkins

Image 42

William Riley Calkins

Image 43

Delbert C. Calkins

Look at the three individuals in images 41, 42, & 43 and compare each of their images. Notice how the genetic traits for the shape of the eyes, shape of the nose, and the shape of the mouth are expressed in both Freeman Calkins and his grandson Delbert C. Calkins. These particular genetic traits seem to have skipped William Riley Calkins, but appear in his child.

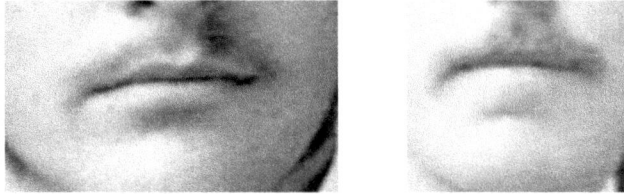

Image 44

Close up of Mouth

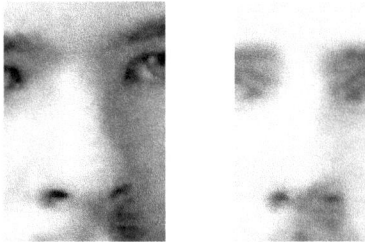

Image 45

Close up of Nose

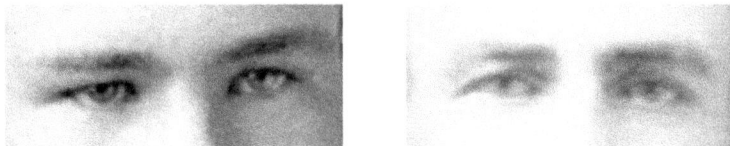

Image 46

Close up of Eyes

Using Principles of Human Heredity on Photograph Identification

Genetic traits from the father can be transferred and expressed in his daughter just like genetic traits from the mother can be transferred and expressed in her son. In this example, the genetic trait for the shape of the eyes found in the father, Elisha Calkins has been transferred to his daughter, Laura H. Calkins, where as the genetic trait for the shape of the eyes found in the mother, Anna Dalrymple has been transferred to her son, Heman Calkins. Here follows a brief description of the lineage of the individuals I will be discussing in this example:

- **Laura H. Calkins & Heman Calkins**, (Author's 3rd great-grandaunt and granduncle)
- **Elisha Calkins** married to **Anna Dalrymple**, parents of **Laura H. Calkins** and **Heman Calkins**.

Who's that Face?

Image 47

Elisha Calkins (Father) & Anna Dalrymple (Mother)

Image 48

Laura H. Calkins (Daughter) & Heman Calkins (Son)

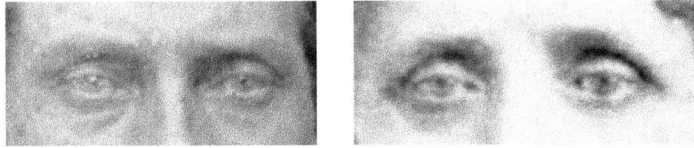

Image 49

Close up of Father and Daughter's Eyes

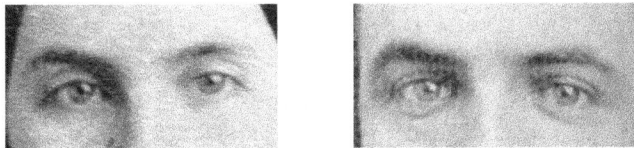

Image 50

Close up of Mother and Son's Eyes

Notice how the shape of each pair of eyes in Image 49 allow for only a small portion of the iris and the white portion of the eye to be visible. On the other hand, the shape of each pair of eyes in Image 50, allow for a larger portion of the iris and the white portion of the eye to be visible. Also there are similarities expressed between the general shapes of the eye socket in both examples.

Factors to consider when observing Photographs

When observing photographs, it is important to remember that not every type of image is the same type or of the same quality, which can lead to difficulty in observing genetic traits of the individuals in each type of image. For example, some images are very old and have unclear images, i.e. blurred faces, where some images are newer with very clean and crisp images. In these newer images, it could be possible to see individual strands of hair or creases in the person's skin. Depending on the type and quality of the image, the degree of difficulty in observing genetic traits of the individual in the image increases. For example when viewing an original Tintype photograph, the image is clear and crisp, but if you view a copy of the Tintype image made by a scanning machine, the image is softer and more fuzzy around each of the features of the person in the image. However, if you view a copy of the Tintype image made by making a photograph of the Tintype image, the image is just as clear and crisp as the original with the features of the person in the image very visible. If possible, it would be best to have an assortment of images of the person you are trying to observe in order to account for the different types and quality of the various images. However, always base your observations of an image with the use of a reference guide photograph or your observations will be meaningless.

Certain factors, such as the type of photographic process used to create the image, age of the photograph, the position of the subject in the image, and the age of the individual, can have an effect on how genetic traits can be observed in photographs. Images have been created for thousands of years, whether being paintings on the walls of caves by prehistoric man or chemical processes resulting in the capture of an image on paper by modern man. With each technique used for capturing the likeness of an individual, there are problems associated with them.

Images created by more artistic measures, such as painting, drawing, or engraving, try to capture the complete essence of the individual, but can result in varying degrees of inaccurate representations of the individual. These artistic measures rely on the ability of the artist and their interpretation of the subject that is sitting in their studio. Even though there are many skilled artists, it would be very difficult for an artist to be able to completely capture every detail in their subject.

Who's that Face?

No two works would be the same, even if the works were of the same subject. Here follows two examples to illustrate this point. The first example focuses on two images of Irving Goodwin Vann, a former Mayor of Syracuse, New York, one of them being an engraving and one of them being a photograph:

Image 51

Irving Goodwin Vann

(Engraving, 1884)

Image 52

Irving Goodwin Vann

(Photograph, 1901)

Image 53

Comparison of Engraving & Photograph

Overall the two images appear to be similar, clearly capturing the essence of the subject. However there appear to be slight differences in the shape of the eyebrows and eyes, and the shape of the chin, but these slight differences, most likely caused by the natural process of aging, do not impact the identity of the individual in the image. The individuals who are represented in Images 51 & 52 are clearly the same person. The second example focuses on two images of Sir Arthur Wellesley, 1st Duke of Ellington, one of them being a portrait painted by Thomas Lawrence in 1814 and one of them being a portrait painted by Francisco Goya between 1812 and 1814:

Image 54

Sir Arthur Wellesley, 1st Duke of Ellington

By Thomas Lawrence, 1814

Using Principles of Human Heredity on Photograph Identification

Image 55

Sir Arthur Wellesley, 1st Duke of Ellington

By Francisco Goya, 1812 – 1814

Image 56

Comparison of Portraits

Who's that Face?

Overall the two images appear to be similar, clearly capturing the essence of the subject. A similarity exists between the two portraits in regards to the shape of the lips, mouth, and chin. However there appear to be differences in the shape of the eyebrows, eyes, and nose. In Image 55 the shape of the eyebrows appear to be more arched, the shape of the eyes appear to be more rounded, and the shape of the nose appear to be more slender. The individuals who are represented in Images 54 & 55 almost look like two different individuals, but when taking into the account of the shape of the lips, mouth, and chin, it is clear that the differences in the shape of the eyebrows, eyes, and nose are attributed to the artist's interpretations of their subject, and that the individual in Images 54 & 55 are the same person.

Images created by more technological processes using any of the various types of camera result in images accurately depicting the individual that is being photographed. With the use of exposing certain chemicals to light, permanent images are able to be transferred to backgrounds made by metal sheets or paper. Most recognizable types of photographic images include Ambrotypes, Daguerreotypes, Tintypes, Carte de Visites (CDVs), and Cabinet Cards. Even though each of these mediums produce images that are more accurate representations of the subjects being photographed, it is important to remember that photographs taken of a single individual from different cameras can result in distortions of the person's image. Each part of the camera was manufactured by hand by skilled craftsmen, with no two parts being identical. For example the lenses used in the cameras were cut, grinded, and polished by hand. If the lenses were made just a fraction off from another one of the other lenses, the image produced would become distorted. For example, think of the mirrors found in a Fun-House at the circus, which can cause the viewer to become very tall and skinny or very short and fat.

Who's that Face?

Image 57

Freeman Calkins (Tintype, 1865)

Image 58

Freeman Calkins (Tintype, 1865 – 1870)

Using Principles of Human Heredity on Photograph Identification

For example, here are two Tintype images of my 3rd great-grandfather Freeman Calkins taken during the middle of the 1860s. Image 57 was taken circa 1865 and Image 58 was taken between 1865 and 1870. Freeman Calkins would be roughly the same age in each of the two images. He is also positioned in a similar manner looking forward, although in image 58, his head is slightly askew. When comparing the two images, it is clear to see that the shape of the head, eyes, and mouth including the moustache are almost identical. These two images clearly represent the same individual.

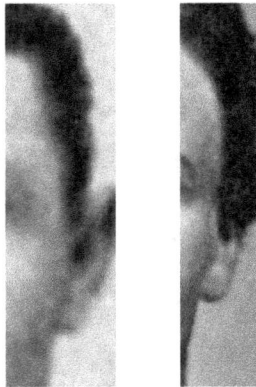

Image 59

Close up of shape towards Top of Skull

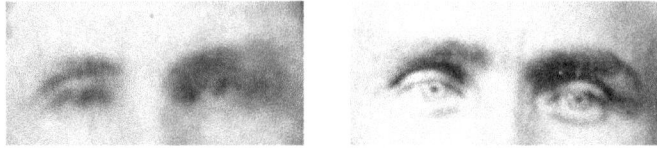

Image 60

Close up of Eyes

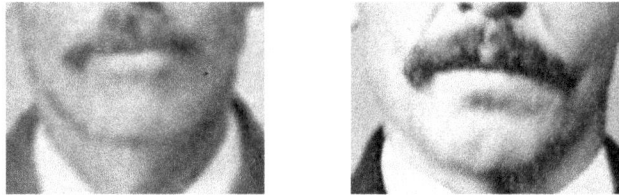

Image 61

Close up of Mouth

However, there are some inconsistencies related to the shape of the nose and individual's right ear. Notice how the shape of the nose in Image 58 is slightly wider than the shape of the nose in Image 57. Also notice how the shape of the right ear is closer to the head with the bottom lobe longer in Image 58, but the shape of the right ear is further from the head with the bottom lobe being more proportional to the rest of the ear in image 57.

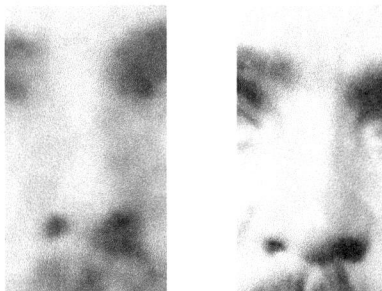

Image 62

Close up of Nose

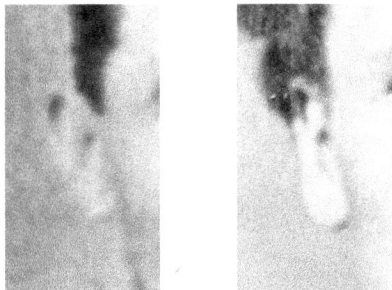

Image 63

Close up of Right Ear

Who's that Face?

These inconsistencies are more likely than not caused by the manufacture process employed, which consisted of individual handcrafting parts such as lenses, in making cameras during this time period.

The most important factor that can have an effect on how genetic traits can be observed in photographs is the age of the individual at the time the photograph was created. As people undergo the process of aging, their bodies perform a wide array of physical changes. As a person develops their various genetic characteristics begin to be expressed. Think of photographs you have seen of yourself as a child, a teenager, and or young adult, just to name a few. Do you look the same in each of those photographs? Similarities between each image of you do exist and can be seen in each of those images, but the fact remains the same, you are different. To illustrate this concept here are a series of photos of Dorman Calkins spanning approximately a twenty year period.

Image 64

Dorman Calkins 1860 (Left) & 1865 (Right)

Image 65

Dorman Calkins 1870 (Left) & 1875 (Right)

Who's that Face?

Image 66

Dorman Calkins 1880 (Left) & Before his death on December 17, 1883 (Right)

Notice the changes in the shape of the eyes and the hair line as the individual ages. The eyes begin to droop, creating an arch-like effect as the individual ages. Also the hair line shows a gradual recessive from the younger images to the older images. The shapes of his nose, lips, and ears stays consistant as he ages.

Using Principles of Human Heredity on Photograph Identification

Another factor that can have an effect on how genetic traits can be observed in photographs is the position of the subject in the image. If the person's head is turned to the right or left, or looking slightly down or up, can impact how the shape of their eyes, ears, nose, mouth, or even the general shape of the head is viewed. To illustrate this point look at your own face in the mirror. Look straight ahead into the mirror and notice how the features in your face look. Now move your head, up, down, left, and right and observe how the features in your face change, when your head is each new position. Some of your features look different and if you did not know that you were looking at yourself, you would probably think that you were looking at a different person. Keep this in mind when you begin to observe genetic traits in individuals found in photographs.

Anyone can do Genealogy

Introduction

What would you say if I told you that you could be a Genealogist? What if I told you that you do not need to have a fancy college degree or an expensive certification to do something that you probably already do on a day to day basis? After all genealogy is one of the most popular indoor hobbies along with stamp collecting and coin collecting. Have you ever wondered what the answers to any of these questions could be:

Who are my parents?

Who were my grandparents?

Who were my great-grandparents?

Where did my ancestors live?

What did my ancestors look like?

What types of jobs did my ancestors have?

Using Principles of Human Heredity on Photograph Identification

If you have posed any of these questions to yourself, then you have already become a genealogist. You might think that a genealogist is a professional person with a bachelor's degree or master's degree and any number of various certifications or credentials, which conducts genealogical research for monetary gains, but that is just not true and a huge misconception. Anybody can do genealogical research and anybody can be a genealogist.

According to the Merriam-Webster online dictionary, a **genealogist** is defined as **a person who traces or studies the descent of persons or families**. Although this is true for a more experienced researcher, a less experienced researcher is working in reverse, since most of the time the person does not know who their oldest known ancestor is. For the above definition to be accurate a genealogist would begin conducting their research with the oldest know ancestor. For example King Henry VIII of England would be the starting point and the genealogist would work downward from him. It is more common for a person to start their research with the earliest known ancestor, themselves.

How to Conduct Your Research

Start with yourself. You are the very top leaf on your family tree and with some time researching, you will be able to see more leaves on the tree along with the roots. Begin by writing down on a piece of paper or start typing up a new word document on your computer what you know about yourself. Include the following items: **Your Name**, **Birth Date**, **Place of Birth**, **Your Father's Name**, and **Your Mother's Name including her Maiden Name**. After writing down these items review additional data, which will help confirm what you already know. Locate your **Birth Certificate**. The original or a copy of the original is what you will need. Review the document and add any additional information that you may have forgotten or did not know previously to your piece of paper or word document. Additional information found on the Birth Certificate could include any of the following items: **Your Father's Occupation**, **Your Father's Age**, **Your Mother's Age**, and **Your Parent's Residential Address**. Reviewing the document will verify the accuracy of what information you have gathered. These starting pieces of information will help guide you as you begin to further your research efforts and your journey as a genealogist. You are now a genealogist.

Continue with your Father or Mother. Now is time to add a few more leaves to the family tree. Once you know the names of your parents, write down the information that you know about them. The information should include **Their Name**, **Birth Date**, **Place of Birth**, **Their Father's Name**, and **Their Mother's Name including her Maiden Name**. Talk to your parents if you are able to. They might be able to provide you with their original Birth Certificate or a copy of the original Birth Certificate. Just like with looking at your own Birth Certificate or a copy of it, you will be able to identify **Your Father's or Mother's name (including their Middle Name)**, **Your Father's or Mother's Birth Date**, **Your Father's or Mother's Place of Birth**, **Your Father's or Mother's Father's (Your Grandfather's) Name**, and **Your Father's or Mother's Mother's (Grandmother's) Name including her Maiden Name** with additional information found on the Birth Certificate including any of the following items: **Your Father's or Mother's Father's (Grandfather's) Occupation**, **Your Father's or Mother's Father's (Grandfather's) Age**, **Your Father's or Mother's Mother's (Grandmother's) Age**, and **Your Father's or Mother's Parent's Residential Address**. Reviewing the document will verify the accuracy of what information you have gathered. If your situation includes one parent or both parents whom have died, obtaining a copy of their **Death Certificate** will help you verify the information you have gathered as well as adding additional information to your genealogical research. By looking at the Death Certificate or a copy of it for one parent or both parents, you will be able to identify **Your Father's or Mother's name (including their Middle Name)**, **Your Father's or Mother's Birth Date**, **Your Father's or Mother's Place of Birth**, **Your Father's or Mother's Father's (Your Grandfather's) Name**, and **Your Father's or Mother's Mother's (Grandmother's) Name including her Maiden Name** with additional information found on the Death Certificate including any of the following items: **Your Father's or Mother's Occupation**, **Your Father's or Mother's Age**, **Your Father's or Mother's Residential Address**, **Your Father's or Mother's Cause of Death, Your Father's or Mother's Next of Kin (usually the Informant of the Death),** and **Your Father's or Mother's Parent's Place of Burial**. Each one of these new pieces of information will help guide you in your next step of your genealogical research. These new pieces of information will also help you when you seem to hit a dead end. They will provide insight into where your next research efforts need to be directed. For example, if you were able to discover the place of burial for your Grandfather or Grandmother, you may want to visit the Church in which the cemetery is located or contact the Church. The Church Staff can search for any records that might pertain to the Individual you are searching for. They may be able to provide you with copies of the Baptismal Register, Confirmation Register, Marriage Register, and Burial Register, which directly contain mention of the person you are searching for. These registers are important when you have successfully researched various family lines for several generations because often there are times in which a family will live in an area for an extended period of time (over a hundred years) and are members of the local church congregation. Several generations of a family can be found in the above mentioned Church Registers. Remember as you successfully find your ancestors Birth Certificates, Marriage Certificates, and Death Certificates may not be available or may not have been in existence and you will have to rely on the various Church Registers for the necessary information.

Continue with your Father or Mother's Father or Mother (Your Grandparents). Now is time to add a few more leaves to the family tree. Once you know the names of your Grandparents, write down the information that you know about them. The information should include **Their Name**, **Birth Date**, **Place of Birth**, **Their Father's Name**, and **Their Mother's Name**

including her Maiden Name. Talk with them if you are able to. If you are unable to do so, then you must now begin searching for information found in other resources. These resources can include the following **Church Registers**, various **Census Records**, **Obituaries printed in various National and Local Newspapers**, **Newspaper Articles**, **Will Records**, **Deed Records**, **Maps**, **Plat Maps**, **Military Records**, various types of **Governmental Records** (Applications for Social Security Cards, Benefits, Visas, etc.), and **Photographs**.

When new pieces of information are found repeat the process for each new piece of information.

Using Principles of Human Heredity on Photograph Identification

Donovan Hurst Books

Check out these other titles available from Donovan Hurst Books:

Alexander Surname: Ireland: 1600s to 1900s by Donovan Hurst

Blundell Surname: Ireland: 1600s to 1900s by Donovan Hurst

Burdett Surname: Ireland: 1600s to 1900s by Donovan Hurst

Carmichael Surname: Ireland: 1600s to 1900s by Donovan Hurst

Crozier Surname: Ireland: 1600s to 1900s by Donovan Hurst

(Also Available in Kindle Format)

Delahoyde Surname: Ireland: 1600s to 1900s by Donovan Hurst

(Also Available in Kindle Format)

Disney Surname: Ireland: 1600s to 1900s by Donovan Hurst

(Also Available in Kindle Format)

Eccles Surname: Ireland: 1600s to 1900s by Donovan Hurst

(Also Available in Kindle Format)

Echlin Surname: Ireland: 1600s to 1900s by Donovan Hurst

Figgis Surname: Ireland: 1600s to 1900s by Donovan Hurst

(Also Available in Kindle Format)

Free Surname: Ireland: 1600s to 1900s by Donovan Hurst

Garrett Surname: Ireland: 1600s to 1900s by Donovan Hurst

Harris Surname: Ireland: 1600s to 1900s by Donovan Hurst

(Also Available in Kindle Format)

Hetherington Surname: Ireland: 1600s to 1900s by Donovan Hurst

Ingham Surname: Ireland: 1600s to 1900s by Donovan Hurst

Jagoe Surname: Ireland: 1600s to 1900s by Donovan Hurst

Knight Surname: Ireland: 1600s to 1900s by Donovan Hurst

L'Estrange Surname: Ireland: 1600s to 1900s by Donovan Hurst

Loftus Surname: Ireland: 1600s to 1900s by Donovan Hurst

Lord Surname: Ireland: 1600s to 1900s by Donovan Hurst

(Also Available in Kindle Format)

Lysaght Surname: Ireland: 1600s to 1900s by Donovan Hurst

Moon Surname: Ireland: 1600s to 1900s by Donovan Hurst

Nerney Surname: Ireland: 1600s to 1900s by Donovan Hurst

Oldham Surname: Ireland: 1600s to 1900s by Donovan Hurst

Paget Surname: Ireland: 1600s to 1900s by Donovan Hurst

Pakenham Surname: Ireland: 1600s to 1900s by Donovan Hurst

Perceval Surname: Ireland: 1600s to 1900s by Donovan Hurst

Rankin Surname: Ireland: 1600s to 1900s by Donovan Hurst

Sale Surname: Ireland: 1600s to 1900s by Donovan Hurst

Seymour Surname: Ireland: 1600s to 1900s by Donovan Hurst

Squire Surname: Ireland: 1600s to 1900s by Donovan Hurst

Tighe Surname: Ireland: 1600s to 1900s by Donovan Hurst

Ussher Surname: Ireland: 1600s to 1900s by Donovan Hurst

Verschoyle Surname: Ireland: 1600s to 1900s by Donovan Hurst

(Also Available in Kindle Format)

Vesey Surname: Ireland: 1600s to 1900s by Donovan Hurst

Wilkins Surname: Ireland: 1600s to 1900s by Donovan Hurst

Woolridge Surname: Ireland: 1600s to 1900s by Donovan Hurst

(Also Available in Kindle Format)

Elisha Calkins & Anna Dalrymple Descendants by Donovan Hurst

Family Photographs of Elisha Calkins & Anna Dalrymple Descendants by Donovan Hurst

Skjerven Gaard Vik Sogn og Fjordane Norway: 1669 to 1922 by Donovan Hurst

Check out this Genealogical Reference Site
Who's that Face?

Checkout this **new genealogical reference site, which allows the researcher to view individuals with the same Surname in order to see the genetic traits of that family name (This is very useful in trying to identify those old family photos). Come see how similar you are to others with the same surname.

Checkout this **new genealogical reference site, which is devoted solely to finding and preserving all types of images, from individual portraits to buildings and landscapes. The site also allows the researcher to view individuals with the same Surname in order to see the genetic traits of that family name (This is very useful in trying to identify those old family photos). Come see how similar you are to others with the same surname.

http://whosthatface.net/

Over 315, 500 photographs and counting

Welcome to Who's that Face?

A genealogical photographic reference collection of vintage photographs from around the world. Building the largest collection of the following types of images: Ambrotypes, Daguerreotypes, Carte de Visite (CDV), Cabinet cards, etc., one picture at a time.

Notes

Notes

Notes

Notes

Notes

Notes

Index

About The Author

Donovan Hurst graduated from San Diego State University with a Bachelor of Arts in the major field of studies of History and a minor in the field of studies of Anthropology. He is a current member of The General Society of Mayflower Descendants and has been conducting genealogical research for over 10 years tracing back his ancestors to their ancestral homelands in Denmark, England, France, Germany, Ireland, Norway, and Scotland.

www.ingramcontent.com/pod-product-compliance
Lightning Source LLC
Chambersburg PA
CBHW080053280326
41934CB00014B/3305